SURVIVAL SKILLS

BEHIND THE SCENES

WRITTEN BY PAUL ROBINSON

CONTENTS

INTRODUCTION TO SURVIVAL SKILLS 4
DAY HIKING 6
NAVIGATION 8
HIKING GEAR 10
FOOD AND DRINK 12
IN AN EMERGENCY 14
SHELTER 16
CAMPFIRE 18

DISCLAIMER:
The activities in this book have been performed by people who are experienced hikers and survivalists, or by people who have had professional training. Neither the publisher nor the author shall be liable for any bodily harm or damage to property whatsoever that may be caused or sustained as a result of conducting any of the activities featured in this book.

Words in **BOLD** can be found in the glossary.

DRINKING IN THE WILD	20	INCREDIBLE SURVIVAL	28
FINDING FOOD	22	GLOSSARY	30
SIGNAL FOR HELP	24	INDEX	31
ALL IN THE MIND	26		

INTRODUCTION TO SURVIVAL SKILLS

Most people live within their comfort zone, seeing the same streets, houses, and faces every day. But it's good to break free once in a while! Hiking through hills and forests can be exciting, but **hikers** need to be prepared.

GOING HIKING

Even something as simple as going for a walk in the country can be risky for people who don't have the knowledge to prepare properly. Hikers must know what to do if weather conditions become more severe than expected, if there are injuries, if the group becomes lost, or if there are any other emergencies.

SURVIVAL KNOW-HOW

Every year, hikers become lost and have to spend the night outdoors. It's important to know what to do in this situation. Survival skills save lives – and not just for hikers! Knowing what to do is essential for anyone – accidents happen, and non-hikers can become stranded in remote areas, such as after a plane crash.

DON'T FORGET!
Never go exploring alone. Always go with a trusted adult, and take supplies and a way of contacting other people in case you get into trouble.

IMPORTANT SURVIVAL SKILLS

There are many different factors that go into surviving the **wilderness**!

SHELTER

FIRE

WATER

FOOD

SIGNALING

DAY HIKING

Hikes can vary in length from a couple of hours to a couple of days, or longer! Going on a day out hiking is popular as it lets people explore an area in a short amount of time. Day hikers often follow circular trails or routes.

SAFETY IN THE WILD

Some people prefer hiking as a pair, and others prefer going in larger groups. Regardless of how many people are going, hikers should always tell someone where they are going and what time they plan to be back. Then, if help is needed, the rescue team knows where to start the search.

PREPARING FOR THE HIKE

Hikers need a few key pieces of equipment for a day's hike. These include a map, a **compass**, water, and food. Other important items are good boots, a hat, and layers of clothing that will keep them warm in the event of an emergency. Sunscreen is also needed in sunny weather.

DID YOU KNOW?

Hikers should always carry **ID** on them that says their name, any medical conditions, and who to contact in an emergency. This is in case they become unconscious, and rescuers need to know key information.

PREPARING FOR SURVIVAL

Nobody plans to get lost, but hikers need to be prepared. They should always carry a survival kit, containing items such as:

- A pocketknife to help build a shelter
- A lighter or matches to light a campfire
- A flashlight to provide light or signal for help
- Whistles, mirrors, or a bright bandanna, which can signal for help
- A first aid kit with dressings, tape, bandages and **antiseptic wipes**

Other useful items include a **bivvy bag**, strong thread, an empty container, water purification tablets, and safety pins.

NAVIGATION

Hikers must have a good map of the area they plan to explore. Even then, it is easy to get lost. The Sun can help – it rises in the east and sets in the west. If hikers walk toward the setting Sun, they know they are headed west.

THE RIGHT EQUIPMENT

Hikers should always carry a map and compass, and know how to use them. Keeping the map in a see-through, waterproof bag helps to keep it dry in rain. If hikers become lost, they should look for features that can be spotted on a map, such as rivers, streams, or hills. A **GPS** can also pinpoint where hikers are on a digital map.

DON'T PANIC!

People who get lost in the wild must stay calm. Groups should never split up to look for help. Staying together, close to the original route, improves the chances of an early rescue.

NEVER AT NIGHT

Trying to walk at night is a very bad idea. It is very easy to slip or fall in the dark, even with the light of a flashlight. Being lost is scary, but being badly hurt is far worse.

DID YOU KNOW?

Young children are told to hug a tree if they get lost in the woods. It's a simple way of staying in one place until they are found. It's harder for rescuers to find somebody who is moving around.

HIKING GEAR

The key to hiking is being prepared for all outcomes. In mountain areas, the weather can change in an instant. It's best for hikers to wear layers of clothes so they can put layers on and take them off to stay the right temperature.

WALKING BOOTS
Boots should be waterproof and cover the ankles to help prevent sprains. They should have a good **tread** to help hikers grip the ground, and cross rocks and difficult **terrains**.

HATS
Hats hold in body heat in cold weather and give shade when it's sunny. Hats help to prevent heatstroke, which causes dizziness, headaches, and vomiting.

SUNGLASSES

It's always important to protect your eyes from the Sun, especially when walking close to water or snow, which are reflective and can make the Sun's rays more damaging to people's eyes.

WATERPROOF JACKET

The jacket a hiker chooses depends on the conditions they expect to hike in. They may choose a thin waterproof for rain showers, or a thicker jacket to stay warm in colder areas.

BANDANNA

A large square of bright cloth has many uses. In cold places, it can be used as a scarf, and in sunny places, it can prevent sunburn. In dusty conditions, a bandanna can be tied over the face for protection.

FOOD AND DRINK

Most hikers eat and drink more when they're out in the wild compared to normal. Climbing hills and walking forest trails burns a lot of energy, so hikers are advised to eat before they're hungry and drink before they're thirsty to keep their body fueled up.

DRINK PLENTY

Most people need 4-8 pints (2-4 liters) of water a day, more if they're doing something active like hiking. Hikers should make sure they carry enough water with them, as it's difficult to find good quality, clean water that's safe to drink in the wild.

TOP TREKKING FOODS

High-energy foods are perfect for a trek into the wild. As hikers must carry all the food they need for their trip, foods that are light but full of nutrients are the best. This includes dried fruit, trail mix, nut-based cereal bars, energy or granola bars, and dried meats or fish.

COOKING IN THE WILD

For short trips, hikers may prefer to take food that can be eaten on the go, without cooking. But for longer hikes, a hot meal can be a real boost. Some hikers build campfires to cook on (in safe places), whereas others may prefer to carry a lightweight stove with them.

TRUE STORY

In 2024, hiker Lukas McClish went missing in the Santa Cruz mountains, USA, during what should have been a 3-hour hike. He survived 10 days without food before being found alive by rescuers.

IN AN EMERGENCY

It's very important to make the right plans and take the right equipment on a wilderness trip. Being prepared helps prevent an emergency situation from turning into a disaster.

ASSESSING THE SITUATION

When hikers get lost in the wilderness, the first thing they need to do is assess the situation. Does anybody know they're missing? How long will it be before somebody comes looking for them? This gives them an idea of how long they have to survive. The next thing to do is build a shelter.

THE NEXT STEP

If they're not going to be rescued for several days, the hiker needs to find water. Most water needs to be purified before it's drunk. In deserts, collecting water may be more important than building a shelter. Finding food is unlikely to ever be a top priority, as humans can survive several weeks without eating.

SURVIVAL PRIORITIES

There is a saying to show survival priorities: you can live three minutes without air, three hours without shelter, three days without water, and thirty days without food.

DID YOU KNOW?

You've probably heard of hypothermia, which is when the body gets too cold. But have you heard of hyperthermia? It's when the body overheats and can't cool down. It's a serious risk for hikers exploring hot climates.

SHELTER

Building a shelter is a top survival skill. Hikers need to know how to build a shelter from the things they can find around them in the wilderness as they might not always have their own equipment with them. Often, the type of shelter will depend on their location.

FOREST SHELTER

A shelter can be made by tying string between two trees and covering it with a **tarp**. Another option is to lean a large fallen branch against a tree trunk, stack branches along the side and cover the frame with leaves. With sloping sides like a tent; this shelter is called a "lean-to".

EARTHY DUGOUT

To build a dugout, find a dry dip in the ground. Hollow it out further then cover it with a tarp or small branches, leaving a gap to get in and out. Use leaves and dirt to cover the shelter.

SNOW CAVE

People lost in the snow should dig a snow cave. A cave that's 3 feet (1 m) deep and 6.5 feet (2 m) long is perfect for one person. Any bigger is difficult to keep warm. There must be an air hole in the roof and the way in should be lower than the rest of the cave. Snow caves are warmer than the icy air outside.

DID YOU KNOW?

Survival is about being resourceful. Hikers can make a shelter out of a plastic bag by cutting a hole for their head and wearing it like a poncho. This keeps body warmth in and rain out.

TRUE STORY

In Colorado, USA, in 1993, a man called Bill Jeracki was out fishing when a boulder fell on his leg. Bill had no shelter and knew he could die. He cut off his leg with a pocketknife to break free!

CAMPFIRE

A campfire gives warmth, a way to boil water to make it safe to drink, heat for cooking, and a means to dry wet clothes. It also keeps wild animals at bay and acts as a signal to show rescuers where you are. This makes it a key survival factor.

BUILDING A FIRE

Hikers always carry fire-starting equipment, like matches, a lighter, or **flint**. Before lighting a campfire, hikers must collect all the wood and stones they'll need. The stones are placed in a ring around the fire to stop it from getting out of control. Campfires should never be left unattended.

SAFETY FIRST

Fire can be dangerous. Campfires can start a **bush** or **forest fire**. The safest place for a fire is on a patch of clear ground, far away from trees, bushes, or other **flammable** objects. Never build a fire on rocks near a river and never take stones from a riverbed – wet rocks that have water inside them can explode when heated!

DID YOU KNOW?

If the ground is very wet or covered with snow, hikers will usually build their fire on top of a base of green logs.

DON'T FORGET!

Never attempt to make, light, or use fire without an adult's assistance. It can be incredibly dangerous as lots can go wrong quickly. Fires must also be properly put out before being left.

DRINKING IN THE WILD

Drinking enough water is good for your mind as well as your body, and you need a clear mind to survive in the wild. It is not safe to drink water straight from rivers, lakes, or streams. Water must be boiled for several minutes to kill germs.

SOURCES OF WATER

Water can be collected in various ways, but the easiest is by finding a river or lake, or by collecting rainwater. In cold climates, snow can be melted to create water too. Never eat snow – melt it and purify it the same way you would with any other natural water.

LIFE OR DEATH

Humans can live up to three or four weeks without food. But without water, humans die in just a few days. Every drop is vital. Well-prepared hikers will have **iodine tablets** which kill germs and make dirty water pure. Cloudy water must turn clear before it is safe to drink.

TRUE STORY

In 2004, Vietnamese fisherman Bui Duc Phuc was lost at sea in his small boat for 14 days. He survived by drinking his own urine and eating a raw sea turtle! This is not normally safe to do, but did help the fisherman survive this emergency situation.

FINDING FOOD

Most people will never need to find their own food in the wild, but it is good for hikers to know what to do in a real life-or-death situation. Catching big animals is hard; people are usually more successful when hunting insects, fish, or small animals like rabbits.

CATCHING A FISH

A fishing line and a few hooks are easy to carry. If hikers don't have these, trapping fish is a good idea. They can use bait to lure the fish into a net. Most freshwater fish are safe to eat once gutted and cooked over a campfire.

HUNTING INSECTS

Insects are easy to find and catch. Unlike other animals, no special equipment is needed to catch insects, making them ideal in survival situations. Insects are great as they're high in protein and fat. Very hairy or brightly colored ones should be avoided though.

NOT EVERYTHING IN THE WILD IS SAFE TO BE EATEN...

POISONOUS PLANTS

Hikers should never eat wild berries – some scientists say up to 90% of white, yellow, and green berries are **poisonous**. Many wild mushrooms are poisonous too. Some poison is so strong that touching them causes illness, and eating them can kill!

Deadly nightshade

DEADLY DISGUISE

Some poisonous plants look identical to **edible** plants, but can be deadly if eaten. A good example is the moonseed plant – its dark fruits look like grapes, but they're poisonous, and can cause seizures and even death!

Moonseed

DON'T FORGET!

Never eat plants or animals in the wild unless you and an adult are absolutely sure they are safe.

DID YOU KNOW?

Many places have rules about what you can **forage** and hunt. Always learn the rules where you are so you can follow them.

SIGNAL FOR HELP

When lost in the wilderness, hikers have to think about how to show rescuers where they are. Rescue teams may be searching on foot, or using planes or helicopters, so trying a few different signals is a good idea.

CATCHING THE EYE

Colorful bags and bandannas can be laid on the ground to catch the eye of rescuers above. Anything shiny can be used for signaling too. People have used silver foil, mirrors, and even the shiny parts of a credit card. Smoke flares are also good, but don't last long, so hikers should be sure rescuers are looking for them before using. Cell phones can be invaluable, but don't rely on being able to get a signal!

TRUE STORY

In 2004, a dog called Brick was lost in a shipwreck off the coast of Alaska, USA. The brave Labrador was found on a frozen island one month later. He used the only help signal he knew... barking!

SOS

The phrase "SOS" is a distress signal that is used around the world. It can be spelled out on the ground using rocks, tree branches, or written in sand to signal rescuers from above. The bigger the letters the better.

BEING HEARD

Most survivors are found by searchers on the ground. That's why a whistle is vital for all hikers. Signal for help with six loud blasts on the whistle, a one-minute silence, then six more blasts. Another option is jumping, waving your arms above your head, and shouting, but this can drain your energy so is best saved until you know help is near.

ALL IN THE MIND

"I will never give up. I will survive." That's the way to think when lost in the wild. Survival skills help people stay alive for days, weeks, even months, but only if they fight every step of the way. Those who stay hopeful are more likely to survive.

BRAIN POWER

It's hard to keep going when you're cold, hungry, thirsty, tired, and perhaps injured. But the most important thing is to not panic. Plan what is needed to survive and how to signal to rescuers. With the right knowledge and skills, a person can survive almost anywhere on Earth.

MENTAL BOOST

Using survival skills in the wild can help people when they go back to real life. Knowing they can cope when the going gets tough gives them a lift. Even if they never need to use their survival skills, knowing they are there makes them feel good.

DID YOU KNOW?

If you hear strange noises in the night in the wild, yell at the top of your voice. If the noise is coming from wild animals, yelling will scare them away. If the noise is coming from rescuers, they will have a better idea of where you are.

TRUE STORY

In 2019, Amanda Eller went for what should have been a 3-hour hike in the Hawaiian forest. She became lost, but survived the 17 days before being found. She says she stayed as positive as she could with the hope that she would be rescued.

INCREDIBLE SURVIVAL

The instinctive need to survive is something all humans have, but few people ever find themselves needing to rely on it. Here are some of the most extreme stories from people who have done impressive things to keep themselves alive in the wilderness.

ONE-HANDED

Aron Ralston was exploring canyons in Utah, USA, in 2003 when a giant boulder smashed his left hand, pinning it to the wall. He was stuck for 5 days, soon running out of food and water. To survive, Aron cut off his forearm! His story has been turned into a movie called *127 Hours*.

7 WEEKS IN A CAVE

In 2017, Liang Yueh and Liu Chun were hiking in Nepal when the weather turned. They fell into a ravine, where they found a cave to shelter in, but they had no way to escape for 7 weeks! Sadly, Liu died 3 days before rescuers found them. Liang was injured and unwell, but alive.

A GIANT SIGN FOR HELP

Carolyn and Rachel Lloyd became lost on a wilderness hike on an island off New Zealand in 2016. They were lost for 4 days in dangerous terrain, with little food and water. They made a giant "HELP" sign out of rocks and branches, which was spotted by rescuers in a helicopter.

A LONG WALK BACK

In 2010, Edward Rosenthal took what was meant to be a short hike in the Californian desert, USA. On the way back to his car, he got lost and ended up stuck in the desert for 6 days. It's thought he walked around 25 miles (40 km) trying to get back to his car!

WHAT IT TAKES TO SURVIVE

It takes mental and physical strength, know-how, and determination to survive these situations. Unfortunately, stories like these don't always end well, even if the hiker has done everything they can to try and survive. Hikers should always be prepared, and take all the precautions they can to prevent getting into difficulty.

GLOSSARY

Antiseptic wipes – small pieces of cloth that contain a chemical which is able to destroy bacteria. They are used to clean cuts and scrapes.

Bivvy bag – a waterproof, drawstring bag, useful as a shelter in an emergency.

Bush fire – an uncontrolled fire in a bush area.

Compass – an instrument with a dial and a magnetized needle that points north, and can be used to find directions.

Edible – something that is safe to be eaten.

Flammable – something that catches fire and burns easily.

Flint – a piece of hard mineral that produces sparks that can start a fire when it is hit against steel.

Forage – to search for, and collect, something from nature, usually food to eat.

Forest fire – an uncontrolled fire in a wooded area.

GPS – a global positioning system – an electronic device that sends out signals so its position can be tracked accurately anywhere in the world.

Hikers – people who enjoy going on long walks in nature.

ID – identification. Usually this is a card which shows someone's name, date of birth, and a photo of their face to prove it's them.

Iodine tablets – tablets that contain the chemical iodine, which can kill bacteria in dirty water and make it safe to drink.

Poisonous – something that contains or produces a substance that can harm, or even kill, a person or animal.

Terrains – stretches of land.

Tarp – a piece of thick waterproof material, often carried by people who spend time outdoors.

Tread – the bottom part of the shoe or boot that touches the ground. It usually has got grooves and patterns in it.

Wilderness – a remote area that is not inhabited by humans.

INDEX

A
Animals 13, 18, 21, 22-23, 27

B
Brick (dog) 24

C
Chun, Liu 28
Cold climates 10-11, 15, 17, 19, 21, 27

D
Daytime hiking 6-7, 12-13, 27, 28

E
Eller, Amanda 27
Emergency 6, 14-15, 21, 24

F
Fire 5, 7, 13, 18-19, 22, 30
Fishing 17, 21
Food 5, 6, 12-13, 15, 21, 22-23, 28, 30

H
Hiking equipment 6-7, 8, 14, 16-17, 18
Hiking gear 6, 10-11
Hot climates 6, 10-11, 15, 28
Hyperthermia 15
Hypothermia 15

J
Jeracki, Bill 17

L
Lloyd, Carolyn and Rachel 28

M
McClish, Lukas 13
Movie *127 Hours* 28

N
Navigation 6, 8-9
Nighttime in the wild 8, 27

P
Phuc, Bui Duc 21
Plants 23

R
Ralston, Aron 28
Rosenthal, Edward 28

S
Safety 6-7, 8
Shelter 5, 7, 14-15, 16-17, 28
Signaling 5, 7, 18, 24-25
Snow 11, 17, 19, 21
SOS 25

T
True stories 13, 17, 21, 24, 27

W
Water 5, 6, 12, 15, 18, 20-21, 28

Y
Yueh, Liang 28

Copyright © 2026 Hungry Tomato Ltd

First published in 2026 by Hungry Tomato Ltd
F15, Old Bakery Studios, Blewetts Wharf, Malpas Road, Truro, Cornwall,
TR1 1QH, UK.

No part of this publication may be reproduced, stored in a retrieval system, or transmitted in any form or by any means, electronic, mechanical, photocopying, recording, or otherwise, without prior written permission of the copyright owner.

A CIP catalog record for this book is available from the British Library.

ISBN 9781835694367

Manufactured in the USA

Discover more at
www.hungrytomato.com

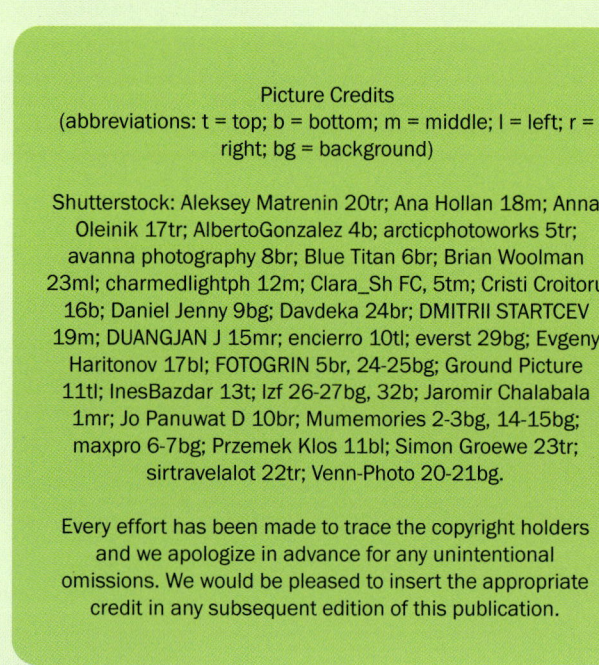

Picture Credits
(abbreviations: t = top; b = bottom; m = middle; l = left; r = right; bg = background)

Shutterstock: Aleksey Matrenin 20tr; Ana Hollan 18m; Anna Oleinik 17tr; AlbertoGonzalez 4b; arcticphotoworks 5tr; avanna photography 8br; Blue Titan 6br; Brian Woolman 23ml; charmedlightph 12m; Clara_Sh FC, 5tm; Cristi Croitoru 16b; Daniel Jenny 9bg; Davdeka 24br; DMITRII STARTCEV 19m; DUANGJAN J 15mr; encierro 10tl; everst 29bg; Evgeny Haritonov 17bl; FOTOGRIN 5br, 24-25bg; Ground Picture 11tl; InesBazdar 13t; Izf 26-27bg, 32b; Jaromir Chalabala 1mr; Jo Panuwat D 10br; Mumemories 2-3bg, 14-15bg; maxpro 6-7bg; Przemek Klos 11bl; Simon Groewe 23tr; sirtravelalot 22tr; Venn-Photo 20-21bg.

Every effort has been made to trace the copyright holders and we apologize in advance for any unintentional omissions. We would be pleased to insert the appropriate credit in any subsequent edition of this publication.